ON THE FARM

Written By

Emilie Dufresne

BookLife
PUBLISHING

©2020
BookLife Publishing Ltd.
King's Lynn
Norfolk PE30 4LS

All rights reserved.
Printed in Malaysia.

A catalogue record for this book is available from the British Library.

ISBN: 978-1-83927-836-5

Written by:
Emilie Dufresne

Edited by:
Robin Twiddy

Designed by:
Danielle Rippengill

All facts, statistics, web addresses and URLs in this book were verified as valid and accurate at time of writing. No responsibility for any changes to external websites or references can be accepted by either the author or publisher.

Sniff! Sniff!

Sniff! Sniff!

Image Credits

All images are courtesy of Shutterstock.com, unless otherwise specified. With thanks to Getty Images, Thinkstock Photo and iStockphoto. Front Cover - Svietlieisha Olena, PremiumVector, Amanita Silvicora. Title typeface used throughout - PremiumVector. 2&4 - What's My Name. 4 - elbud, nlin.nee, Thanakorn Hongphan. 5 - MR.PRAWET THADTHIAM. 6&7 - NordStock. 7 - Eric Isselee, Tsekhmister. 8 - Aleksandra Saveljeva. 9 - siam sompunya, Viktorija Reuta. 10&11 - Olga_DigitalWork. 11 - Csanad Kiss, Eric Isselee, stockphoto mania. 12 - rtbilder. 13 - MyImages, Micha, Michele Paccione, curiosity. 14&15 - M Kun. 15 - Eric Isselee, Csanad Kiss, Tsekhmister. 16 - N-sky. 17 - O.PASH, Tiia Monto [CC BY-SA 3.0 (https://creativecommons.org/licenses/by-sa/3.0)], Studio Ayutaka, Jennifer Gottschalk. 18&19 - charnsitr. 19 - Eric Isselee, photomaster, yevgeniy11. 20 - Aneta Jungerova. 21 - MyImages - Micha, MSSA, Magicleaf. 22 - stockphoto mania, Kritsada.S. 23 - photomaster, viewsphotos.

CONTENTS

Words that look like **this** can be found in the glossary on page 24.

ALL ABOUT POO

Hard and round, squidgy and soft, or runny and watery...
Poo comes in all different shapes and sizes depending
on lots of different things such as **diet** and **digestion**.

Animal poo might also
be called droppings,
manure or faeces.

Don't touch any poo you find on the farm. Poo has lots of nasty things in it!

On the next page you will see some poo on the farm. Read all about the poo and then, from the three animals, choose whose poo you think it is. Turn the page to see if you were right!

GIANT AND GRASSY

Wow – this is a big one! But whose poo is it?

Sniff, sniff! This poo doesn't smell too bad – the animal probably eats lots of <u>fibre</u> and green things.

The poo is in ball shapes that seem to have squashed when it dropped from a height.

WHOSE POO WAS IT?

It was the **horse's POO!**

It was me all along! I'm a big animal and I make big poos!

A horse eats around ten kilograms of hay every day. That's the same as eating over 14 loaves of bread a day!

In a year, a horse can make nine tonnes of poo. That's about the same weight as Tyrannosaurus rex!

Horses eat a lot. This means they poo a lot – around ten times every day!

Horses are <u>herbivores</u>. This means they eat lots of plants which have many parts that can't be digested.

9

SPLATTERED AND FLAT

Watch your step – it's a wet one! But whose poo is it?

This poo is very wet and has the <u>texture</u> of porridge.

It is piled in a disc shape and is around three centimetres tall.

WHOSE POO WAS IT?

It was the **cow's POO!**

Alright, it was me! Now let me get back to eating — I have to graze for eight hours every day...

BURP

During a cow's digestion, it produces a lot of gas which is bad for the environment. But this doesn't just come out as farts - it comes out as burps as well!

Cows have to 'chew the cud', which means they bring up the food they have eaten back into their mouths to chew it for longer. This helps with digestion.

A cow's poo is runnier than other herbivores' poo. It forms a puddle on the floor.

A cow's stomach has four parts, unlike humans, dogs and horses who only have one part.

What an unusual shape these droppings are. Whose poo could it be?

This poo is shaped like small pellets and some have been squished together.

This poo is smooth and <u>uniform</u>, without bits in it – similar to cow poo.

Whose poo could this be?
Choose from these three animals.

This animal probably grazes throughout the day.

There are lots of trails and piles of this poo across the field.

Sheep

Pig

It doesn't smell like one of mine...

Sheep dog

15

WHOSE POO WAS IT?

It was the sheep's POO!

Oh, was it me? I hadn't even noticed. I poo all day long.

Sheep chew the cud like cows do. This makes their poo smooth and uniform.

Sheep can poo and eat at the same time!

Sheep eat and poo throughout the day so there are lots of pellets everywhere.

Sheep stand up and walk around when they poo. They might also wag their tails to spread their poo farther.

17

FIRM AND FOUL

Get your nose pegs – it's a stinker! But whose poo is it?

The poo is in a long log shape and is a chocolate-brown colour.

This poo smells quite bad.

Whose poo could this be?
Choose from these three animals.

There are clumps of grass and mud around this poo. This animal probably kicks and scrapes the ground after pooing.

The poo has the texture of wet modelling clay.

Goat

Sheep dog

Pew! That stinks!

Pig

19

WHOSE POO WAS IT?

It was the dog's POO!

It was mine all along! I kicked up those pieces of grass and mud too!

Dogs scrape and kick the ground with their back legs to fling mud and grass. This helps to cover the poo up and mark their territory.

21

BONUS POO!

WHITE WEES

Chickens, like other birds, don't wee like humans do. Instead, their wee comes out as white-coloured waste along with the rest of their poo!

Poo

Wee

POO-SPLOSION!

Lots of farmers have big problems with pig poo. If pig poo is left alone, it can explode without warning!

A pig can make around five kilograms of poo every day. That's around ten times as much as a human poos!

Did I do that?

GLOSSARY

carnivores	animals that eat other animals instead of plants
diet	the kinds of food that a person or animal usually eats
digestion	the journey that food takes through the body where it is broken down and important things are taken out to be used
environment	the natural world
fibre	a part of some foods that takes longer for animals to break down
gas	a thing that is like air, which spreads out to fill any space available
graze	eat grass and other plants in a field
herbivores	animals that only eat plants
processed	when food is changed in some way to make it taste better or last longer
territory	an area that an animal thinks to be its own
texture	the look or feel of something
uniform	having the same size and shape throughout

INDEX